The Battle

Lewes

1264

Maria Caulfield

Acknowledgements

Photos, illustrations and maps are by the publisher except:
Tomb of Simon de Montfort - Smb1001 : Richard of Cornwall captured - Jon Edgar :
Fletching - Charlesdrakew : Lewes Castle barbican - Charlesdrakew : Lewes Cliffe
Hight Street - Editor5807 : Lewes Priory - Top Cat 14 : Tonbridge Castle - Clem

Website - www.BretwaldaBooks.com
Twitter - @Bretwaldabooks
Facebook - Bretwalda Books
Blog - bretwaldabooks.blogspot.co.uk/

First Published 2014
Text Copyright © Maria Caulfield 2014
Photos, maps and illustrations Copyright © Bretwalda Books 2014, unless otherwise stated
Maria Caulfield asserts her moral rights to be regarded as the author of this work.

Bretwalda Books
Unit 8, Fir Tree Close, Epsom,
Surrey KT17 3LD
info@BretwaldaBooks.com
www.BretwaldaBooks.com
ISBN 978-1-909698-96-3

CONTENTS

Preface

The impact and significance of the Battle of Lewes, whilst celebrated and remembered locally, often goes underplayed by national historians. Unusually at the time the battle was not about gaining land or wealth but was fought on the principle of getting better, fairer government and resulted in Britain's first ever representative parliament. My interest in writing this book came initially from a political stance rather than a military one because as a local nurse who is standing for Parliament, I owe a great deal to the outcome of this battle.

In the year of the 750th anniversary of the Battle of Lewes, this book reminds us of how hard generations before us have fought for our democracy and freedom and if things had turned out differently, how easily democracy may have escaped us. At a time when many people are disillusioned with politics and politicians, the Battle of Lewes illustrates how precious our freedom to choose those who represent us in Parliament really is. Britain as a nation – and in fact most of the Western World – owes a great debt to those who fought on the battlefields of Lewes that day.

My aim in writing this book is to highlight the motives behind the battle and identify the key people and stages involved. What fascinates me about this battle in particular is how at each and every stage the battle could have been so easily won or lost. Personalities seemed to play a huge part in the battle itself and really influenced the final outcome rather than military tactics. The book also underlines how short lived the success of those involved was with Simon De Montford being killed in battle within the year.

Ultimately the book is a short guide to the battle because while the people of Lewes are very familiar with the tale, outside of the town the story about the day which changed the history of this country remains largely unknown.

A huge thanks go to Rupert Matthews and all at Bretwalda for their help and support and to the people of Lewes for keeping the story alive.

Maria Caulfield

Chapter 1
The Barons' War

The dispute that led to bloodshed at Lewes on a beautiful spring day in 1264 originated with King Henry III's determined insistence that he had the sole right to rule England as he wished, combined with his utter inability to do so competently - or indeed at all. If he had been less autocratic or more competent his reign may have passed by peaceably, but as it was civil war wracked the kingdom. But out of that bloodbath was born the foundations of the democracy that England, Britain and many parts of the world have gone on to enjoy.

Time after time Henry raised taxes for one purpose, then spent the money on something else. He went to war without consulting his nobles, but then expected them to muster the men he needed. He lavished money on the Church, and saw no reason to object when that money was spirited out of England to fund lavish lifestyles for prelates in Rome. An early sign that the nobles were not going to take all this lying down came in 1243 when Papal Legate Martin travelled to Shropshire to find out why taxes levied by the Pope had not been paid.

A local magnate named Fulk FitzWarin listened to the legate, then replied "I tell you to go, leave this land at once."

"What is your authority to give orders to the legate of the Holy Father?" demanded the outraged Martin. For reply FitzWarin drew his sword and laid its point at Martin's throat. Martin left without his money.

Such incidents were at first few, scattered and local, but in 1258 events moved to the national stage. Henry had lost an unnecessary war with France, then launched an invasion of Wales that was called off before the army even crossed the border. Both military adventures had been expensive, but even more so was Henry's ambition to make his brother Richard, Earl of Cornwall, the Holy Roman Emperor and his younger son Edmund the King of Sicily.

At this date a new Emperor was elected when the old one died. The electorate was restricted to the seven most powerful noblemen in the Holy Roman Empire: the Princes of Cologne, Mainz, the Palatinate, Bohemia, Saxony, Brandenburg and Trier. Previously there had usually been an obvious heir or strong candidate and the election had been something of a formality, but when Frederick II died in 1250 there was no clear front runner, so numerous ambitious nobles eyed up the imperial crown. Through his wife, Sanchia of Provence, Richard was related to several important families in the Empire and fancied his chances, especially as he had recently been on Crusade and came back with a fine reputation. In the event it turned out the princes wanted cold hard cash in return for their votes, and Richard persuaded Henry to pay the vast sum of 28,000 gold marks only for the

King Henry III, who ruled England from 1216 to 1272.

election to end in deadlock. Richard was crowned King of the Romans, but never managed to gain the Imperial throne.

The Kingdom of Sicily proved to be equally elusive. The Pope knew Henry wanted an inheritance for young Edmund and offered to sell him the throne of Sicily. Henry paid a massive price demanded by Pope Innocent IV, but there was a catch - or rather two. First the kingdom was to be held as a feudal fief of the Papacy, meaning that much of the wealth of the kingdom went directly to Rome. Second there was already a King of Sicily in the shape of Conrad Hohenstaufen and he had no intention of making way for Edmund. It transpired that Conrad was in dispute with the Pope, who had declared him to be dethroned though without the power to remove him from power. Henry had paid a fortune for an empty claim.

All of this cost more than Henry could afford and by 1258 he was effectively bankrupt. He summoned the barons to meet him at Oxford and asked them for more money and higher taxes. The barons agreed, but laid down strict conditions that became known as the Provisions of Oxford. Although the Provisions contained many clauses, the key ones stated that the king had to dismiss all his foreign advisers and could spend no money without the agreement of a Council of 15 barons. Henry reluctantly agreed, and swore holy oaths to implement the new rules. It was an attempt to curb the absolute power of the monarch, but only by allowing the barons a say. The rest of the country had to be content with trusting the barons to help the king appoint honest sheriffs and other officials.

This came at a time when society and economic power across Europe was changing. For centuries wealth came from land, from the crops and livestock that could be raised there. Political power was in the hands of the landowners who had the wealth. Gradually, however, that was changing. More and more money was to be made by trading or manufacturing. As yet the merchants produced only a minority of the kingdom's wealth, but it was a steadily growing minority. And that fact that merchant's wealth tended to be in the form of ready cash, while the wealth of barons was all too often tied up as livestock or grain made the merchant's wealth more valuable to a king for it could be taxed or borrowed more easily. Of course, the merchants were not nobles, nor even knights, they were mere commoners and so no higher up the social scale than peasants, but their money gave them confidence and they began to aspire to have some say in how their taxes were spent.

Meanwhile the barons were falling out among themselves. Now that they had

The Provisions of Oxford are presented to King Henry III by Simon de Montfort and his fellow barons in 1258.

acquired more power they found that the did not always agree and some of the disputes about how to govern England grew heated. In 1262 Henry gained absolution from the new Pope Urban IV that meant he no longer needed to abide by the holy oaths he had given the barons. He repudiated the Provisions of Oxford, sacked the officials appointed by the barons and put his own men in place.

8

In 1263 riots by Londoners supporting the cause of reform forced Queen Eleanor, wife of King Henry III, to flee the city. As she passed under London Bridge in a barge the angry citizens threw rubbish at her, one chamber pot full of filth landing on her head. This insult to royal dignity angered the royalists and had much to do with the savage vengeance that they would later take on the rebel leader, Simon de Montfort, Earl of Leicester.

The barons gathered to rebel, and Henry submitted the matter to King Louis IX to arbitrate. It was merely a delaying ploy for Louis was bound to find that his fellow monarch had the right to rule his own kingdom.

One powerful baron spoke out loudly against Henry. This was Simon de Montfort, Earl of Leicester, who was married to Henry's sister Eleanor. Other barons spoke in terms of feudal dues and baronial power, but Simon spoke in terms of what was right, what was moral and what was just. Men who paid taxes had a right to know how that money was spent. Men subjected to the law had a right to know that the law was applied fairly and equally. Men who obeyed the king had a right to know that the king ruled wisely. Some of the greater barons were none too certain about all this, realising that what applied to the king would also apply to themselves, but the knights and the merchants loved it.

King Henry was in the Tower of London with is wife Eleanor and son Edward when Londoners launched a loud and noisy demonstration supporting de Montfort. Fearing rebellion, Henry put Queen Eleanor in a boat and ordered the crew to row her upstream to Windsor Castle where he had a strong garrison. As the boat passed under London Bridge the apprentice boys showered it with rubbish, and the contents of a chamber pot splattered on the queen's dress. Young Prince Edward was furious and vowed revenge on the Londoners.

Long talks followed between the king and de Montfort, but nothing was achieved except that barons and cities shifted in their opinions and allegiances as the discussions dragged on. Trouble flared at Rochester in Kent when the castle's commander John de Warenne, Earl of Surrey, who supported the king, insulted Gilbert de Clare, Earl of Gloucester, who favoured de Montfort. Gloucester rode off to his own castle at Tonbridge, and on 17 April came back to lay siege to Rochester. De Montfort rode out of London with a small force to help Gloucester.

The news that the issue had turned to war spread across England like wildfire. Everywhere men rushed to take sides and grab weapons. Apart from Gloucester, the greater barons mostly sided with Henry, while the lesser nobles, knights and merchants backed de Montfort.

Henry and Edward moved rapidly to secure the main fortresses of the Midlands, then headed for London where men supporting de Montfort were gathering. Realising that London was too strong for them to take the royal pair then swung south to take Gloucester's castle of Tonbridge and swept on to capture his other stronghold at Kingston in Kent. Gloucester's wife, Alice, was in Kingston when the castle fell to the royal army, but Henry let her go unharmed. The royal army then lunged toward Rochester, forcing de Montfort and Gloucester to call off the siege and head back to London. It was only a feint, for Henry marched rapidly to Hastings to make sure he had control of a major port before marching west along the coast apparently heading for the West Country. It had been a lightning campaign by medieval standards, and one that put de Montfort and Gloucester at a serious disadvantage.

The campaign was not over yet. King Henry was marching fast, accompanied now by his son Edward and his brother Richard, Earl of Cornwall and King of the Romans. His route was taking him to the Sussex town of Lewes.

Chapter 2
Commanders at Lewes

Henry III commanded the royal army in person. He was aged 57 and had seen plenty of military action. Unfortunately little of it had been successful and his contemporaries generally blamed him for the failures. In 1230 he invaded France to try to reclaim lands confiscated by the King of France, but the campaign descended into farce as Henry marched fruitlessly between failed sieges. He agreed a truce in 1234. There was intermittent warfare with Llewellyn the Last of Wales, the campaigns being dominated by raid, ambush and patrols. Henry at first poured in resources, but he had no real plan of campaign and agreed a truce that was broken and patched up several times. War with France broke out again in 1241 and Henry marched an army to near disaster at Taillebourg. Total slaughter of king and his army was avoided only by a skilful rearguard action fought by Richard of Cornwall, Henry's younger brother. Perhaps chastened by the close shave Henry thereafter preferred diplomacy in his relations with Wales, Scotland, Ireland and France to war. Lewes was his first taste of actual warfare in more than 20 years.

Prince Edward was the eldest son of King Henry. He was young, rash and at times hot-tempered, but he was also clever and able to act subtly when he wanted to do so. He generally opposed the reforms championed by Simon de Montfort, not for their own sake but because they were being forced upon the Lord's anointed monarch by a bunch of rebellious nobles. Always ruthlessly determined to stamp out rebellion, he was equally able to see the need for reform and urged several of de Montfort's ideas on his father.

As a military man Edward had some experience. As well as the usual training to be expected of a medieval royal prince, Edward had commanded an army campaigning in Wales in 1262. He asked his father for men and advice when the Welsh raided his lands near the border, but Henry replied only "What is it to me? The land is yours. Take action, win fame when you are young and make your enemies fear you. For me, I am busy with other matters." Short of men and money

Edward did his best. He drove the raiders back and made limited reprisals. He had fought no major battle before Lewes, but he had learned much about keeping a force supplied in field, about keeping up morale in difficult situations and about the need for reconnaissance. In the heat of battle at Lewes he was to forget all these lessons and meet with disaster, but he never forgot them again.

Richard, Earl of Cornwall, was the younger brother of King Henry and one of the most experienced military commanders on the field at Lewes. He was born in 1209 and as a young man was granted extensive lands by his brother. In 1238 he fell out with Simon de Montfort as he opposed Simon marrying his sister, but was placated by gifts from his brother. He went on Crusade in 1240, earning a solid reputation for military skill although he fought in no major battles. His brother Henry endowed him with Poitou and Gascony, ancestral lands in France that had been lost to the French crown so although Richard had titles, he did not have the lands to go with them. He spent some years campaigning in France to win the estranged lands but, although he did well Richard never had the resources

The seal used by Richard of Cornwall to confirm documents, agreements and charters. It shows him in true chivalric pose, mounted on his charger and riding into battle.

The seal used by John de Warenne, Earl of Surrey, clearly shows the blue and gold chequed coat of arms used by the Warenne family.

he needed to make conquest a reality. There then followed Henry's efforts to get him the thrones of Sicily and the Empire, which were to lead to such high taxes and alienate so many people in England from Richard. When Henry got into trouble at home, Richard came back from Germany to lend his support and proved to be a valuable military adviser in the months leading up to Lewes.

John de Warenne, 6th Earl of Surrey, was aged 33 at Lewes and like all noblemen had been trained in the business of fighting and commanding an army. His ancestor, William de Warenne, fought at the Battle of Hastings in 1066 with William the Conqueror and shared in the spoils of victory. This William was created Earl of Surrey in 1088 and given extensive lands, among them the town of Lewes where he built a castle and founded a priory. The lands and titles passed through the generations to John who was an early friend of Prince Edward, although he was a few years older than the prince. In 1247 he married King Henry's half-sister Alice of Lusignan, who despite her royal links was virtually penniless.

Thereafter Surrey remained close to Prince Edward and at first backed the king against the reforming barons. In the later 1250s, however, Surrey joined the voices of those calling for reform and agreed with the Provisions of Oxford. He was still backing reform in 1263, but was steadfastly against taking up arms against the king. It was an injudicious remark of Surrey, by 1264 Constable of Rochester Castle, that led the more outspoken reformer the Earl of Gloucester to unsheathe his sword and lay siege to Rochester, thus starting the civil war that led to Lewes.

Surrey conducted the defence of Rochester with determination and courage, though his skill has been called into question. Much of the town went up in flames before he and his men retreated to the castle, where the royal hall also burned to the ground. The outer bailey then fell to the rebels and Surrey was holed up with his men in the keep. This was an immensely strong structure and resisted the stones hurled at it by the siege engines brought up by Gloucester. After a week of the keep standing alone, the siege was suddenly lifted as a royal army approached.

Surrey then marched his men out, leaving behind a small garrison, and joined the king for the march across Kent and Sussex to Lewes.

Simon de Montfort was the leader of the reformist army at the Battle of Lewes. He was born in France in 1208 as the son of another Simon de Montfort, a famous crusader. His grandmother had been the heiress to the Earldom of Leicester, which brought with it extensive lands in England, but these had been forfeit to King John many years earlier. Simon got his elder brother to renounce his nominal

A relief of Simon de Montfort, Earl of Leicester, attached to the modern battle monument at Lewes in Sussex, the scene of his greatest victory. Henry of Almain had become a sworn enemy of de Montfort and all he stood for by 1266, having jeered at de Montfort's corpse at Evesham.

claim to the English title and lands and went to England to try his luck. He found that the Earldom of Leicester and its lands were held by the aging and childless Ranulf, Earl of Chester. By a mix of charm, tact and deal-making Simon persuaded Ranulf to leave him the old Leicester inheritance, and gained the title from King Henry III in return for persuading his brother to renounce other claims to English estates. In 1239 Simon de Montfort therefore became Earl of Leicester and a wealthy man.

In Leicester de Montfort met Robert Grosseteste, Archdeacon of Leicester Abbey, who was a noted scholar, devout Christian and champion of honesty and fairness in public office. Grosseteste had already acquired a reputation for cracking down on corruption and assorted abuses within the Church and would soon embark on a vociferous campaign to enforce similarly high standards among royal officials. There can be no doubt that it was Grosseteste who enthused Simon de Montfort with similar ideas.

Simon de Montfort had meanwhile been making himself agreeable to King Henry III and in 1238 he married the king's sister, Eleanor. This was a slightly awkward move since Eleanor had earlier taken a holy vow of eternal chastity to avoid a marriage she had not wanted. Simon went on a pilgrimage to Rome to make amends and made his peace with the Pope in return for a cash payment, but the papacy never really forgave him for having - as the Church saw it - debauched a holy virgin.

In 1239 Simon quarrelled with King Henry over a sum of money that Simon owed to the King's uncle, but had not paid. He fled to France with his wife. Simon left Eleanor in France with relatives while he himself went on Crusade. He returned in 1241 having won a solid reputation for competence in military matters, but without having actually fought a battle against the Moslems. Hearing that Henry III was fighting a campaign against Louis IX of France in Poitou, Simon dashed there to join the English army and so regain royal favour.

Back in England, de Montfort gradually became exasperated at Henry's incompetent rule. For many years he favoured trying to reform the situation by pointing out the problems to the king and persuading him to appoint competent and honest officials, but eventually he became convinced that the real problem was Henry himself. In 1258 he supported the Provisions of Oxford as a way to restore sound government, but spoke out against the fact that only the nobles had a role under the new regime and that both Church and commoners were excluded.

By the time of the Battle of Lewes, Simon de Montfort had seen more military campaigning than any of the other commanders on the field. He had fought in the Holy Land and in France. He had led large bodies of men on the march, keeping them fed and watered and not asking too much of them by way of distance covered nor imposing too harsh or too lax a discipline. He had not fought in any major battles, but had commanded numerous small skirmishes and minor sieges so he knew his business well enough.

Henry de Montfort, eldest son of Simon de Montfort, was aged 26 in 1264. In the years of dispute between King Henry III and the barons, Henry acted as a messenger for his father. He travelled extensively and got to know many of the key nobles of the land, as well as establishing links with wealthy merchants and the ruling councils in the bigger cities. He seems to have been a popular and engaging young man who made friends easily. In January 1264 he travelled to France to act as spokesman for his father to King Louis IX while the French king was arbitrating the dispute between King Henry and his barons. It was almost certainly a message sent by Henry that alerted Simon de Montfort to the fact that Louis's decision was a foregone conclusion in favour of Henry.

On his return to England, Henry was given a small body of troops and sent to the Welsh Marches to secure towns and castles for the cause of reform. Civil war had not broken out at this point, so Henry's mission was more to raise money and secure supporters in official positions than anything else. He took Worcester and Gloucester, but then found Prince Edward was approaching on a similar mission but with a larger force of men. Since neither Henry nor Edward wanted to be the first to draw their swords in the dispute, the two men met on outwardly friendly terms and agreed that Henry would retire to his family's castle of Kenilworth while Edward travelled the Marches.

Henry had barely got back to Kenilworth when he heard that war had broken out at Rochester. He mounted up and led his men to London where he joined his father for the march to Lewes.

Guy de Montfort, third son of Simon de Montfort, was 22 at the time of the battle. Almost nothing is known of his life up to this point. Presumably he had undergone the standard military training of a young nobleman and so was competent to be jointly in charge of a part of his father's army at Lewes.

Gilbert de Clare, 7th Earl of Gloucester, was the only major noble who came out openly to support de Montfort and his reform movement in the crucial spring of 1264. He was widely known as The Red Earl due to the strikingly red colour of his hair, which formed an unruly mop on top of his head. Gloucester was a young man in 1264, only 21 years old and had inherited his earldom and his estates just two years earlier on the death of his father. Like all noblemen he had been trained from a young age to fight as a knight and to command any army in times of war as well as to administer his estates in years of peace - the roles expected of a medieval nobleman.

Although Gloucester was young and inexperienced he was a man to be reckoned with for he was not only enormously wealthy but also came from one of the oldest and most respected noble families in England. His ancestor Richard fitz Gilbert de Clare took part in the Norman invasion of England in 1066 and was rewarded by William the Conqueror with huge estates, 176 lordships and the prestigious right to build his own castle at Clare in Suffolk, from which he took his title. The family grew in stature in the years that followed, acquiring the title Earl of Gloucester by marriage in 1180 and with it extensive lands in the Welsh Marches.

He rallied to de Montfort's cause early on and stuck with it despite overtures from both Henry and Edward. As the armies converged on Lewes Gloucester was one of the few men who seemed eager to fight against his king.

Tonbridge Castle in Kent was one of the first targets for the Royal army. It belonged to leading rebel noble the Earl of Gloucester and commanded a vital crossing point on the upper River Medway. The Gatehouse, shown here, had been completed only four years earlier.

Chapter 3
Men Weapons and Tactics

A t the time the Battle of Lewes was fought, Europe was still very much a feudal society. The heart of the feudal society was an economic-military deal in which a king or nobleman granted a temporary lease on land to another man in return for service. The economic underpinning of the entire system was at the very bottom of the social pyramid where land was given to peasants in return for a set number of days labour in the landlord's fields in the course of the year. This freed the landlord from the need to do any actual work himself and allowed him to concentrate on other tasks instead.

Some land holders were abbeys or cathedrals or monasteries who contributed to society in other ways, but the vast majority were laymen and their task was to fight. It is with them that we are concerned here.

Although there were variations, land was usually parcelled out in what were known as "knight's fees", that is the amount of land needed to generate income to support a knight and allow him to be able to afford a warhorse, a riding horse and the arms, armour and supplies that he needed to go to war.

Each knight had to serve for a set number of days each year in return for his fee. This was usually between 40 and 60 days and though the lord could ask the knight to serve for longer the knight could refuse and, if he agreed, expected to be paid. It also seems to have been the case that while the knight was expected to feed himself and suffer the cost of any lost or damaged equipment during his first 40 or 60 days of service, once he was being paid the lord had to keep him supplied and replace anything that got or damaged - including the horse.

War horses were extremely expensive animals at this date costing perhaps five or six times as much as a riding horse. The cost was not so much due to the type of horse, for war horses were only slightly larger than riding horses, but to the training. A war horse had to have the stamina to go on long marches, often with only sparse or poor quality fodder. And once into battle, the war horse had to remain calm and obedient without being timid or scared. Moreover it was expected to be able to carry out a wide range of moves unknown to other horses. It had to rear up and stomp on men on command, kick backwards at other horses or turn around in its own length. Only a minority of horses were able to do these things, and those that could took years to train. No wonder a horse was a knight's most valued piece of equipment.

Some knights did not go on campaign, but were instead allocated to castle guard duty. This had the advantage of being carried out close to home, but usually lasted longer with 3 months being the average. Castle guard duty did not always involve manning a castle, it might refer to commanding a town militia to guard a town or other garrison tasks. It has been conjectured that older knights or those suffering long term wounds stood castle guard, but this is by no means certain.

Not all knight's fees were held by knights. Some fees were handed to two sergeants instead of a single knight. A sergeant at this date was a mounted soldier who lacked the heavy armour and well trained war horse of a knight. This meant he was not as much use in a battle, but he was invaluable on campaign. To sergeants fell the tasks of patrols, skirmishing, riding ahead to seize bridges, securing food supplies and grabbing hapless peasants to question them about enemy troop movements.

Sergeants would usually invest in a metal helmet, but their body armour tended to be of boiled leather or gambeson, a type of heavy quilted fabric firmly stuffed with wool or old cloth.

Some knight's fees were divided in other ways, providing four infantrymen, for example.

Just as not all knight's fees provided knights to the army, not all of them took the form of land. A knight's fee might be an annual cash payment, or perhaps the right to levy import or export duties at a small port. Almost anything in the gift of a king or lord might comprise a knight's fee. In theory none of these fees were hereditary, but by the 13th century in practice they were. All a son and heir had to do was pay a sum to the lord and he inherited his father's lands, and his duties.

It is thought that in the 13th century England was divided into about 7,000 knight's fees of land with another 1,000 or 1,500 knight's fees taking the form of non-land fees.

Of course, no king would divide all his lands up into individual knight's fees and distribute them himself. In the days before writing was a common skill and government bureaucracy was non-existent such a system would not work. Instead a ruler tended to hand large numbers of knight's fees to great nobles, who then parcelled them out to lesser nobles who in turn gave them to individual knights, sergeants and so forth.

This form of feudalism was the system that the Normans imported to England when they conquered the kingdom in 1066. However, in England there were three key factors not found on the continent that the Normans kept and which made England unique. First was the concept that many people paid a cash sum instead of rendering service. For military duties this payment was known as "scutage", meaning "shield money" and equated to the sum needed to pay a mercenary to do the duty instead. By the 13th century it is thought that the majority of knight's fees in England paid scutage instead of performing service.

The second feature was that every able bodied freeman (that is not slaves or serfs) aged between 16 and 60 had to turn out armed and ready for local defence. This obligation was traditionally limited to the shire where the person lived and lasted only as long as an enemy army was in the shire. This formed the basis of the local militias of England. In the mid-13th century the development of these was still in flux but it seems that already a community would band together to afford the equipment of a man chosen, or volunteering, to go to war. The militiamen would later become well-trained and valuable part-time soldiers, but in the 1260s most were still amateurs able only to perform second rank duties.

The third key feature of military service in England was that every man right down the chain of feudal obligations even down to the lowest serf or slave owed allegiance and loyalty to the king. The intermediate nobles and knights were merely agents of the king. On the continent each person owed allegiance only to their immediate superior, so if a nobleman rebelled against his king all his feudal adherents were obliged to join the rebellion.

In England the loyalty to the king tended to put a brake on rebellions and made civil wars much less frequent and less widespread than on the continent. When Simon de Montfort led his uprising he claimed that he was raising troops on behalf of the king in order to rescue him from the influence of foreign and wicked advisers. It was not true, of course, but it was a necessary legal fiction to persuade men to join his rebellion.

The size of units raised under the feudal system varied enormously. One nobleman might bring two knights, four sergeants and half a dozen infantrymen with him to war, others would have several hundred of each. Such units served under their feudal superior and often resented being sent off on detached duty. It was generally easier for a commander to send off a junior nobleman with a small retinue to do a task than to ask a great magnate to divide his force. All of which made command structure on the battlefield somewhat complex.

The various ranks of noblemen expected to be treated with the honour due their rank, irrespective of how many men they commanded or how experienced they were at war. Thus a king had to give commands to an earl before a baron, and to a baron before a knight. A commander might find himself in the awkward position of having to give orders to a young, untried earl while an experienced baron with a large contingent hung about in the background. In most instances tact and understanding could get around such issues, but not always.

Mention has been made of mercenaries. This term today has negative connotations, but in the 13th century being a mercenary was an honourable and honest profession that attracted men from all levels of society. Even the great nobles might spend time as a mercenary before inheriting their estates and the responsibilities that went with them.

Mercenaries served for cash payments. Although those sums were usually expressed in daily terms - 24 pennies for a knight, 12 pennies for a sergeant and two pennies for a foot soldier were typical - contracts were usually negotiated for a fixed term of months. At this date there were no permanent mercenary bands or armies as would come later, but there were famous mercenary captains who knew where and how to recruit surprisingly large numbers of men at short notice. Mercenaries serving in England tended to be German, French or Breton. They were armed and equipped in much the same way as English fighting men.

This heavily armoured knight wears an iron helmet padded with leather over a mail coif. This type of helmet first appeared about 1140 and remained very common through to around 1270. The heraldic charge on his shield is repeated on the side of the helmet. The mail hauberk reaches to his knees. His mail leggings reach from above the knee to the toes. His right arm is covered in mail, with a mail gauntlet. The left arm, protected by the shield, lacks mail. His lance is not shown, but his long sword hangs from his belt.

21

Elsewhere in Europe there were specialised troops skilled at certain types of fighting - such as the Basque mercenaries adept at mountain warfare - but they seem to have been absent from England.

Mercenaries were much better disciplined, better trained and better equipped than a feudal army. As a result they were popular with kings, but they were expensive and because they demanded payment in cash in a society where most taxes and business deals were done in kind even rich men could not always pay them. Mercenaries were, in theory, organised in units of 10 and 100 men, with larger mercenary armies being composed of units of 100.

The reputation of medieval warfare has suffered in recent years. It is often supposed that medieval battles were little more than disorganised scrummages of murderous violence carried out by ignorant men possessed of little more than brute force and big swords. This was very far from being the case. Medieval warfare had a surprisingly complex range of tactics and manoeuvres on which a commander could call. Admittedly only the well trained mercenaries could be relied upon to carry this out reliably and with precision, the less professional feudal soldiers might attempt such manoeuvres but in the heat of battle with enemies pressing in they could not always be relied upon to do so successfully.

The basic infantry tactic was the shield wall. This was composed of several ranks of men, usually 8 or so deep, standing shoulder to shoulder. They presented their overlapping shields to the enemy to form a solid wall of shields - hence the

This figure is wearing the sort of equipment to which town and county militia aspired, but rarely achieved. Mercenaries, however, would have worn such equipment as a matter of course. His helmet is of iron, padded inside with a thick leather lining stuffed with wool. The mail hauberk has a coif under the helmet and reaches to the thighs and elbows. Over the hauberk he wears a sleeveless tunic made of thick leather on to which have been sewn overlapping scales made from horn. The lower legs and arms are bare of armour. His triangular shield is about 30 inches tall and 24 inches wide and is made of thin, overlapping sheets of wood faced with boiled leather stretched to fit and then left to harden. His main weapon is a 10 foot long thrusting spear, with a sword as back up.

name of the formation. Good men could move about the battlefield at a jog and still maintain formation, though most preferred to walk and even then might have to stop every now and then to get back into shape.

Most infantrymen came armed with a spear, which was used to stab at the enemy over the top of a shield wall, but others came to war with axes, swords or bows. There seems to have been little effort made to separate out these men. They all formed up in the shield wall as a mixed mass of different weaponry, presumably with all the men from one area choosing to stand together.

The basic cavalry tactic was the charge, delivered by two or three ranks of horsemen riding knee to knee. Each rank was 20 or so yards behind the one in front so that if a horse fell those behind stood a chance of jumping over it or veering out the way before they too were brought down. A charge of armoured knights delivered at the right time was devastating. Choosing when to launch this charge was perhaps the most important decision a 13th century commander had to make. Well formed infantry could withstand a charge for no horse will gallop straight into a solid object - including a wall of men. But even the slightest disorder would cause a formation to crack under the impact of a charge. Poorly trained infantry would often simply run away in the face of a charge of knights.

And once an army was fragmented and fleeing a commander would find it very difficult indeed to restore order and discipline.

The figure on which this man is based is described as a Londoner in the manuscript where he appears, but he is typical of the sort of man who would be recruited by any medieval army in large numbers. He is equipped with a metal helmet, padded inside with wool and leather and with a kite-shaped shield that covers him from shoulder to knee. His main weapon is a short thrusting spear and he would have had a heavy knife or small hatchet tucked into his belt as a reserve weapon. In action these men formed up shoulder to shoulder with their shields overlapping to form a solid wall of shields facing the enemy. Whether a unit of such men would be able to carry out any of the more sophisticated battle tactics of this period would depend on their level of training.

Chapter 4
The Battle of Lewes

The royal army straggled into Lewes on 6 May. Henry was in no great hurry for events were going his way and in any case most of the knights were riding horses tired out by the marathon march to Rochester. With Tonbridge and Hastings taken and Rochester relieved, Kent was now firmly in the grip of the Royalist forces.

One chronicler tells us that Henry chose to rest at Lewes while waiting for reinforcements that were on their way from the Midlands. Whatever the reason, rest Henry did and Lewes was a good place to do it. The town was small but prosperous and surrounded by a defensive wall which, if not exactly state of the art, was strong enough. It also occupied a strategic location, the importance of which is not immediately obvious today. In 1264 the estuary of the River Ouse reached right up to Lewes and sea-going ships could dock at the town. By staying in Lewes, Henry could maintain communication by sea with his supporters in the Midlands and the North as well as staying in touch with the supportive King Louis IX of France and Pope Urban IV. At the same time the South Downs provided good routes to both east and west and the Ouse Valley was the site of a good road running north to London.

But Lewes was not only a good centre of communications, it was also secure and comfortable. Lewes Castle was considerably stronger having two mottes and a central bailey, all defended by stone walls and towers. It was, moreover, the ancestral home of John de Warenne, 6th Earl of Surrey, a long term friend of Prince Edward. There was, therefore, little to fear from treachery among the garrison or servants at the castle who if they were not loyal to the king would be loyal to the earl. Unsurprisingly Edward settled into the home of his old boyhood pal and relaxed.

Facing page: The barbican entrance to Lewes Castle. The castle was not only strong, but was also the ancestral home of the Warenne family and so a secure base for the Royal army.

King Henry, meanwhile, took up lodgings in Lewes Priory. Henry knew what he was doing for this was one of the largest, most lavish and most comfortable priories in England. It had been founded in 1081 by the same William de Warenne who had established Lewes Castle and by 1264 had amassed vast estates not only in Sussex but also in Norfolk and the Midlands. The priory church was one of the largest in England, bigger than most cathedrals, while the park and gardens were more than large enough to contain the entire royal camp. The park wall was not as strong as a proper defensive town wall would be, but it did at least serve to keep the men contained and meant that access to the town and its taverns was limited to those with permission to go.

Henry was an experienced commander and either when he first arrived, or soon afterwards, he sent out scouts and posted patrols around the town. A key point was the village of Offham to the north. It was here that the high chalk hills of the South Downs closed in on the banks of the River Ouse to form a narrow valley with steep sided hills rising over 300 feet on either side. Lewes itself stood at the southern end of this defile, a mile or so south of Offham. The road ran alongside the river through the valley so any traveller coming from the north would have to pass Offham to reach Lewes.

On 12 May a messenger from Simon de Montfort presented himself at the gates of Lewes with a message for the King. Reading the letter today it appears to be a solid testimony of baronial allegiance to a feudal lord, but appearances can be deceptive. In fact, de Montfort and his allies had spent a considerable amount of time drafting the letter with a firm eye on how it would be received when, as was certain, it was passed to other barons and other monarchs around Europe. After the usual salutations the letter affirms the absolute loyalty of de Montfort and his supporters to Henry and to royal government. The sting comes next when de Montfort asks the king to abide by the Provisions of Oxford, says that he does not trust "certain persons among those who surround you" and states that he has armed men with him for the sole purpose of "resisting attacks from those persons who are not only our enemies but also yours". The letter then concludes with more assurances of loyalty and the customary closing salutations.

Henry for one was not deceived. He knew that among the "certain persons" was his own brother Richard, Earl of Cornwall, and his wife's uncle Boniface, Archbishop of Canterbury. These were men he relied upon enormously to help with the business of government. Criticism of them and their actions was criticism of the king's government and therefore, in Henry's eyes, of the king himself.

Unlike the barons, the king spent no time at all drafting a careful message. He sent for a clerk and striding the hall of Lewes Priory in a fit of anger he dictated a short, terse reply that ended "We therefore value not your faith nor love and defy you as our enemies."

As the messenger was about to leave, Richard of Cornwall and the young Prince Edward pushed into his hands another hastily written note that they had both signed. It read "We let you know that you are all defied as public enemies by each and all of us your enemies and that henceforth whenever occasion offers we will with all our might labour to damage your persons and properties."

When he read these two angry notes de Montfort could be in no doubt that bloodshed was now inevitable. He did not delay in making his preparations.

Within minutes of receiving the replies from Lewes, de Montfort rode south with a small force of horsemen to scout out the land between himself and the king. He rode down the valley of the Ouse, on the west side of the river, without incident until he reached the village of Offham. Here he ran into the patrol posted there by Henry and a sharp little skirmish took place. The fight appears to have taken place west of the main road where a narrow coombe cuts into the towering Offham Hill behind what is now the Blacksmith's Arms public house. Perhaps the royal patrol was camped in this little valley from which they could watch the road and river without being seen by anyone approaching from the north.

The outcome of the skirmish is not recorded, but its importance lies in the fact that this was the first time that Henry realised that de Montfort and his army were nearby. After Rochester de Montfort had been seen heading towards London, and that was the last definite news that Henry had of his whereabouts. In fact de Montfort had stayed in London until 6 May, when a messenger came in from Hastings. Presumably the messenger came to report that the king and his army had marched through the town, but he must have said something else as well for de Montfort was galvanised into frantic activity. Within hours he had his army on the march towards Hastings. Somewhere near Sevenoaks de Montfort learned that Henry had marched on to Lewes, so he veered southwest and hurried toward that town. He got to the village of Fletching on 8 May, having covered over 50 miles in less than three days. This was very fast marching indeed for the period, when a distance of 12 miles was considered a good day's march. We do not know the reason for de Montfort's haste, but when he reached Fletching he learned Henry was stationary at Lewes so he too set up camp and waited until the 12th to send his message to Henry.

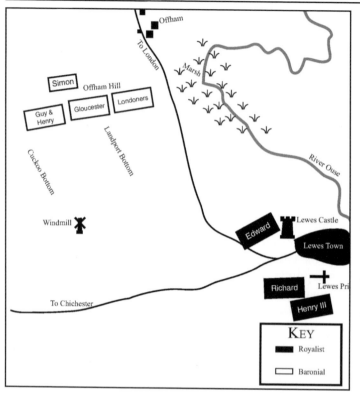

At about 9am the army of Simon de Montfort was drawn up on Offham Hill, having surprised the Royal lookouts. Prince Edward had his cavalry drawn up in front of Lewes Castle, but Henry III and his brother Richard of Cornwall were slow forming up their men.

Now that he was aware that de Montfort's army was close by, though not exactly where it was, Henry took the usual precautions of a medieval commander close to an enemy. He sent men to watch all the approach routes that a hostile army could take and ordered his men to be ready for instant action by keeping their weapons and armour close to them at all times. Beyond that, however, Henry did nothing. He made no efforts to find de Montfort's army nor to fortify Lewes. Instead he summoned his clerks and took care of some routine government business. Prince Edward retired to Lewes Castle where he seems to have had a jolly good dinner with his host William de Warenne.

The king's lack of urgency seems to have rubbed off on his men. Certainly the scouts sent up to the top of Offham Hill to watch the approaches from the north fell asleep. The first that these unfortunate men knew that events were moving fast was when they were awoke shortly after dawn to find themselves surrounded by grinning rebels prodding them with wickedly sharp lances. The hapless lookouts were quickly tied up and cast aside. They were to get a grandstand view of what was to follow.

De Montfort's army had left their camp near Fletching at dawn, with the fast riding advanced scouts reaching Offham Hill around 5am. It was not until about 7am that the bulk of the army reached the hill. They had marched down the road to Offham, then turned right to climb up on to the high ground. The reason for the move was clear. From his reconnaissance the previous day Simon knew that the narrow defile on the banks of the Ouse itself would be virtually impossible to force against even a small force.

In any case, one chronicler tells us, Simon did not intend to launch a surprise attack on the king. Perhaps he still hoped for some peaceful resolution before serious amounts of killing took place. Or perhaps he had decided that if a fight had to take place it should take place on ground of his own choosing where his lack of mounted knights would not be such a drawback. If so, he chose his ground well.

There may have been more to it than that. Besieging a castle is one thing, but actually drawing your sword in the presence of the annointed king is quite another. Many nobles and knights had shown themselves to be very uneasy about joining a rebellion, no matter how much they despised the king and his officials. De Montfort must have suspected that if he attacked the king he would alienate those of his supporters who were uncertain about the legality or morality of civil war. But if the king attacked him first then de Montfort could plead that he acted in self defence. The drafting of the letter sent to Lewes had been undertaken especially to show that the rebels were prepared to go out of their way to try to find a peaceful solution.

Simon de Montfort deployed his army on the crest of Offham Hill from where he could look down on Lewes. The left flank of this position rested on the cliff-like slope that dropped precipitously down to the River Ouse. The right flank, a thousand yards from the left, rested on the slopes of Cuckoo Bottom. These were not quite so steep as those falling to the river, but they were too steep for cavalry and that was what mattered most. The land between the two was almost flat, ideal for the deployment of an army. To the south a long, fairly gentle slope ran down to Lewes, up which the royal army would need to advance if it were to attack. Behind his position the land varied. To the west, at the right of de Montfort's army, the land rose another 70 feet or so to peak at Mount Harry before falling down to the lowlands at Allington. At the east, or left end, of de Montfort's position the line was backed by the steep sided coombe in which the skirmish of the previous day had taken place. The buildings of the now closed Lewes Racecourse stand in front of the centre of the line taken by de Montfort's army.

De Montfort divided his army into four divisions. The first was under the command of his two youngers sons, Henry and Guy. This division was put on the right. The central division was commanded by the Earl of Gloucester. On the left were arrayed the Londoners. Nobody at the time thought to record who commanded them, so presumably the city's men were commanded by some local knight of no great social importance. The final division was under the command of Simon de Montfort himself. The precise position where it was put is difficult to work out from contemporary records, but it was probably on the slopes leading up to Mount Harry from where de Montfort could watch events unfold. As so

The ruins of Lewes Priory. In 1264 this was one of thelargest prirories in England, with ample space for the Royal army to camp in the grounds and luxurious guest quarters in which King Henry III could stay.

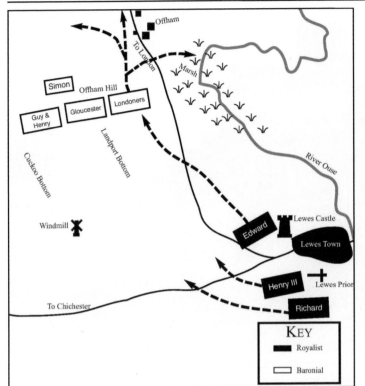

At around 10am, the timings of this battle are only approximate, Prine Edward led his knights in a headlong charge that swept the Londoners from the field. But Edward gave chase, leaving his father and uncle to attack the remainder of the Barons' army.

often with medieval battles it can be difficult to be certain about numbers. However, it is likely that de Montfort had about 5,000 men with him on Offham Hill. Of these barely 400 were mounted knights, and those he kept in his own reserve. The three divisions of the front line were all on foot. With everything in place, de Montfort told his men to eat the breakfast they had carried with them. They had been on the move since dawn and there was no sign of the royalist army as yet.

De Montfort had brought with him from Fletching what contemporaries describe as being his "chariot". The nature of this vehicle has been the subject of some dispute. It is known that de Montfort had broken his leg a few months earlier, and had not yet fully recovered. Long hours of riding brought on considerable discomfort, so he travelled in the "chariot" whenever he could. It also carried his letters, records and the materials for writing more. The fact that it was singled out by contemporaries for comment must mean that it was

Fletching, ten miles north of Lewes. Simon de Montfort camped his army here while he scouted ahead for places to offer battle and while he sent messages to the king.

something unusual, not the sort of light two-wheeled pony cart used by most knights or militia on campaign. Presumably, therefore, it was more of a four-wheeled cart of the type used by nobles when travelling with their household in peacetime. Also with de Montfort's army was the bulk of their baggage, mostly transported in pony carts or on pack horses. All this was left in or near Offham together with the boys, cooks, craftsmen and others who accompanied a medieval army on the march. Simon left them a small guard, but it does not seem to have amounted to more than a few dozen men.

The Royal scouts on Offham Hill may have been asleep, but not everyone was so relaxed. Several of the grooms caring for the horses of the knights with Prince Edward were out at dawn cutting grass to take back to feed their charges. They saw the hostile army deploying on the high ground and raced back to Lewes

Castle to tell the knights who employed them. They in turn told Prince Edward who dashed up to the castle battlements to see for himself. It was now about 8am or so.

Edward recognised the enemy army for what it was and sent a messenger scurrying south to the Priory to alert King Henry while he himself got the knights and mounted men at arms in the castle ready to enter the fray. In fact Henry was alerted by the sounds of Edward's trumpeters sounding the blasts that summoned the knights billeted in castle and town to his banner - "They loudly poured forth a terrible sound" wrote one chronicler. From the priory Henry could not see the rebel army, the slight rise on which Lewes town stood was in the way, but he must have realised straight away that the enemy was approaching and it was only minutes before Edward's messenger arrived.

Henry at once mustered his men for battle. The walls around the priory and the few gates that gave access had seemed a good idea when making camp, but now they imposed a crucial delay. It took time for the men to file out through the gates, then array themselves in their various units.

Then the King's Standard had to be unfurled. At this date the King of England used a banner quite unlike that of other monarchs and nobles. It was a rather curious affair that seems to be descended from the draco standards of ancient Rome. Mounted on top of a pole was a silver dragon's head wet with sapphires for eyes. The mouth of the dragon was wide open to let in the wind and from the rear of the head flowed a long silken tube which behaved rather like a modern windsock. The Kings of England had inherited the banner from the Kings of Wessex, who had used a white fabric for the body and tail of the dragon, who had in turn presumably inherited the design from Rome. Usually there was a quite a bit of ceremonial attached to unfurling the royal banner for battle, but this seems to have been dispensed with as Henry was in a hurry.

Presumably according to a predetermined plan, Henry divided his men into two commands. That on the left was commanded by his brother Richard, Earl of Cornwall, while he himself commanded that on the right. Once formed up the men from the priory marched around the west side of Lewes town to join Edward's men who had formed up immediately north of the town. If this move had been completed properly Edward's force would have formed the right wing of the united royal army, with Henry in the centre and Richard on the left. It was not to be.

Edward was aged only 24 and was famously rash and hotheaded. He was

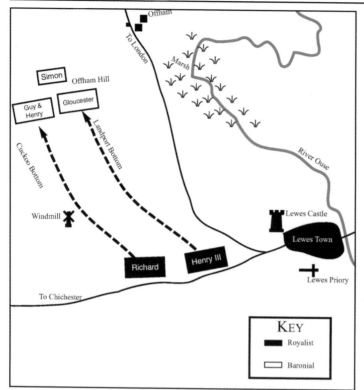

Henry III and Richard of Cornwell led their divisions up the long slope out of Lewes toward Simon de Montfort's forces on Offham Hill. Henry's route was flat at first, but ended in a steeper slope while Richard faced a longer, shallower slope.

surrounded by hundreds of equally young and confident knights. Ahead of him he could see some 5,000 men, most of them infantry, forming up. He had around 2,000 knights and mounted men at arms under his immediate command, and the king was coming up with another 8,000 men. To Edward the battle must have seemed a foregone conclusion.

Moreover he had a personal grudge to settle with the Londoners after the way they had treated his beloved mother a few months earlier. He would have been able to recognise the distinctive striped outfits of the London militia on the left of de Montfort's line and may have guessed that the other men mixed in with them were also Londoners. Edward would also have been able to see that the Londoners were not as well formed up as the rest of de Montfort's army. All the contemporaries agree that the bulk of the Londoners present were ordinary men, not part of the militia. They were not trained soldiers and this would have been obvious to Edward. He must have been itching to get to grips with the Londoners, and his father was taking what seemed an inordinately long time to come forward.

While the Royal army was getting itself deployed, de Montfort rode up and down his lines repeating time and again a short speech to enthuse his troops. According to one account he said "Oh, my beloved comrades and followers. We are about to fight for the government of England and to keep our faith. Let us implore the Lord of all that if it be His pleasure He will grant us strength and help so that we might show grateful service by our knightly belt, overcoming the malice of all enemies." When he had finished, de Montfort strode out in front of his army, threw himself flat on the ground with his arms outstretched to form a cross and shouted "Lord give us victory in Your name." He then mounted his horse, put on his helmet and put himself at the head of his division in reserve.

Down below outside the gates of Lewes Castle, Edward's patience snapped.

Lewes Cliffe High Street on the east bank of the Ouse. The streets of Lewes became a slaughter yard as the Baronial forces hacked to death any Royalists that they could find hiding in the town.

He ordered his knights and men at arms to advance up the hill toward the enemy. With all the panoply of chivalric warfare, the knights advanced at the walk in a solid mass of horsemen. Edward kept the marshes that fringed the river to his right, passing over the firmer land now occupied by Wallands Park housing estate and the Offham Road. Any sensible cavalry commander will avoid a steep slope if he possibly can, so Edward would probably have led his men up the gentler slope that lies north of what is now Highdown Road. Moving at a steady trot, Edward and his men would have covered the distance from the gates of the castle to the upper slopes of Offham Hill in about 10 minutes.

Edward seems to have been about halfway up the slope, perhaps passing near to what is now Gundreda Road, when Henry and Richard of Cornwall finally led their men around Lewes and into sight. Seeing his son advancing to the attack with the bulk of his elite knights, Henry decided to attack immediately. Perhaps hoping to stick to the prearranged plan, Henry advanced on a track to the left of the line taken by Edward. This took him up the steeper slope of Landport Bottom, while Richard of Cornwall took the gentlest slope of all up past a now vanished windmill toward the spot now occupied by the racecourse buildings. The bulk of Henry's and Richard's men were infantry, so they moved more slowly than did Edward. They would have been barely a quarter of the way up the hill when Edward's knights spurred their horses into a gallop for the final few yards and crashed into the Londoners.

As Edward had hoped, the battle was over almost as soon as it began. Trained militia might be able to withstand a charge of mounted knights under the right conditions, but most of the Londoners were untrained and Edward's knights were the elite fighting men of England. Within seconds the knights were hacking their way into the massed ranks of London infantry. Lances smashed into chests, bloodied swords rose and fell - and within minutes the Londoners in the rear ranks decided to get out while they could. As the rear ranks began to beak away and flee, those further forward found themselves without support from behind and faced by the murderous horsemen in front. They too fled and soon the whole mass of Londoners was streaming north, pursued by Edward's mounted knights.

They had not gone more than a few yards before they started down the increasingly steep slope that fell some 300 feet down to Offham. At first the slope was not too steep, but it got steeper toward the bottom and the men going down it were rapidly out of control and many of them were off their feet. Few horsemen could hold their seats going down that slope, and though Edward's knights trained in the saddle for hours every day they were encumbered by heavy armour and engaged in the adrenalin-fuelled business of attacking their enemies. Many of them will have come off their horses as they slithered down the slope. All sense of military formation was smashed and broken long before the thousands of men hit the bottom of the slope.

Once there, the Londoners fled in all directions. Some went east into the marshes around Hamsey or swam the Ouse, hoping the armoured horsemen could not follow them there, others bolted north the way they had come to Chailey and Newick. One man, it was later said, did not stop running until he was hammering on the doors of St Paul's Cathedral begging for holy sanctuary. The knights gave chase, mounted cavalry rarely being able to resist the temptation of the easy kills to be had among a fleeing enemy on foot. Some knights rode for four miles before they drew rein.

Long before that Edward himself had had enough and was urging his

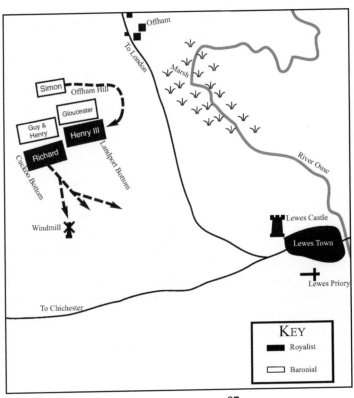

After getting on for an hour of fighting on the hilltop, Richard of Cornwall's division began to fall back and then to retreat back down the slope. Simon de Montfort chose this moment to launch his few mounted knights at the King's division. The charge was the turning point in the battle.

trumpeters to rally the men to his banner. He did not have much luck. Not only were there fleeing men to be butchered, there was also the rebel baggage to be plundered. De Montfort's "chariot" was found and along with it four obviously very wealthy men. These were royalist merchants from London that de Montfort had forced to come with him to act as go-betweens in case the king refused to meet rebel messengers. The men, not unnaturally, objected to being plundered by the army they supported, and were promptly killed for their trouble. Although bloody, the incident was a small one but it does show the excitable, undisciplined and savage mood of the knights that Edward was trying to get under control.

Back on top of Offham Hill, the battle was continuing. As Edward and his men vanished over the hillcrest they passed out of the sight of the rest of the royal army. Neither Henry nor Richard had any idea of what Edward was up to. They must have hoped that, sooner rather than later, he would rally his men and return to attack the rest of the rebels from the rear. That, at least, would seem to be the case if we are to judge by their behaviour.

Simon de Montfort was in a better position to know what Edward was up to. He watched as the confused mass of men from both sides tumbled down the steep hill to Offham, then saw them scatter north and east as the deadly chase went on. He too knew that Edward would be back, but unlike the king he knew that the royal knights would not be back for some time.

Richard of Cornwall had a gentler slope to climb so he and his men assaulted the right wing of de Montfort's army while Henry was still struggling up the steep slope out of Landport Bottom. Richard's men struck the division led by the younger de Montforts hard, but they were tired by the long march up the slope from Lewes Priory. They failed to break through the rebel line, so the fighting settled down to the bloody slogging match that dominated so many medieval battles. The fighting had been continuing for some minutes when the king's division arrived. Henry paused a moment to let his men catch their breath, then charged forward. He too failed to break through and again the ranks hacked and butchered each other at close quarters.

After a while the men of Richard of Cornwall's division began to give ground. The retreat was imperceptibly slow at first, but gradually it speeded up. The king's division remained solid, but both its flanks were now exposed. De Montfort chose this moment to lead his reserve into action. The move proved to be decisive. We do not know quite where the reserve struck, but its intervention was clearly crucial. The cohesion of the royal army was disrupted, at least for a time.

Gloucester's men were able to penetrate the king's division and break up its formation. The majestic aura of royalty, however, remained strong. Nobody wanted to attack the king himself, and Henry's royal presence seems to have been rallying his men. Gloucester knew something had to be done, but also knew that lifting his sword to the king was likely to be counterproductive even in the heat of battle. Instead he attacked the king's horse, slashing at its legs and bringing it tumbling to the ground. Henry was on his feet instantly, and was quickly hustled away by his supporters. He was found another horse, and as soon as he had remounted he reorganised his division.

The royal army now began a long fighting retreat back down the hill up which they had advanced. Henry and Richard must by now have been wondering where Edward and the bulk of the royal knights had got to. It must have been nearly an hour since Edward had chased the Londoners over the crest of the hill and by all the conventions of warfare he should by now have come back to complete the defeat of the rebels. And yet there was no sign of him and it was the royal army that was in retreat and facing disaster.

That disaster was not long in coming. Richard's division collapsed first. At some point during the retreat down the hill the formation gave way and the units fragmented as the men fled for the safety of the priory walls or the town. Richard of Cornwall himself together with a handful of knights took refuge in the windmill that they had passed during their advance.

The king's division continued its retreat. Apparently it got back to the priory in reasonably good order, though with heavy losses. Some units had become separated, and other men had fled to follow the fugitives from Richard's division. De Montfort led most of his men in slow pursuit of the king and then surrounded the priory to prevent his escape. Other units were in hot pursuit of the fugitives. Royalists ran through the streets of the Lewes, trying to get to the bridge and over the Ouse. The men who hunted them were in no mood for mercy and blood was soon flowing down the gutters of Lewes town centre.

Back at the windmill, a group of de Montfort's men had realised who they had cornered and began chanting "Come out, you bad miller." Then they began shouting jokes about millers at the cornered earl, and perhaps a contemporary ribald song concerning a miller's daughter followed. There were no knights or nobles among the baying mob, so Richard of Cornwall wisely decided to stay put. He knew that he was deeply unpopular and, rightly, was blamed by the common people for the high taxes that they had been forced to pay. Looking out across the slopes around the mill that were strewn with his dead and dying comrades, Richard must have feared what his fate would be if he did come out.

Eventually the noise and commotion attracted the attention of the Earl of Gloucester. He rode over to find out what was going on. Finding out that it was Richard of Cornwall who was in the mill, Gloucester pushed through the mob, silenced them and took control. He promised Richard that his life was safe, whereupon the beleaguered Cornwall rather gingerly came down from the mill. Gloucester was as good as his word and took Cornwall to de Montfort, who had

A scene from the battle monument in the grounds of the Priory shows Richard of Cornwall being escorted away from the windmill as the prisoner of the Earl of Gloucester, though in reality Richard was not bound as shown here.

him put under armed guard and sent first to London and then to Kenilworth Castle where was put into comfortable but very secure imprisonment.

It was at this point, perhaps around 2pm but certainly some time after noon, that a large body of armoured knights rode into view to the north. The banners and flags showed that this was Edward and the 1,500 or so knights and men at arms that he had managed to rally to his banner. De Montfort at once gathered his troops together, though he was unable to rally all those hunting the fugitives. Leaving enough men to keep King Henry bottled up in the priory, he drew up his army ready to do battle once again.

For long tense minutes de Montfort and his men stared northward to see what the royal knights would do. Professional knights in full armour were potent fighting men, and Edward had enough of them to still stand a reasonable chance of defeating de Montfort. But the royal knights did not see things that way. Unknown to de Montfort, Edward was in the midst of a blazing row with his

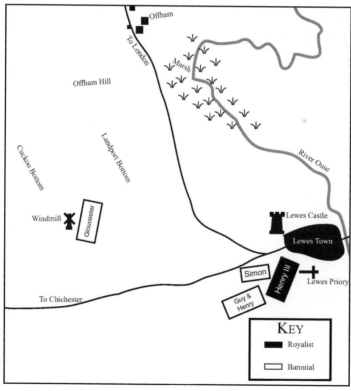

By early afternoon the battle was effectively over. Henry III with the small force he had managed to keep together was barricaed in the Priory, surrounded by the de Montforts. Gloucester was seeking to get Richard of Cornwall to come out of the windmill where he had taken refuge.

leading knights. Edward wanted to advance, charge and scatter the rebels. Most of the knights did not. They could recognise a lost battle when they saw one and knew that it would not be long before de Montfort's mounted men were out securing the surroundings.

Many of Edward's knights did not wait for the end of the argument. They began drifting away, first in ones and twos and then in groups of a dozen or more. The longer Edward argued the case for an attack, the fewer men he had with which to carry one out. Eventually Edward realised the futility of what he was doing. Much to de Montfort's relief the force of knights turned around and trotted away out of sight to the north.

Edward, however, did not go far. Along with a small number of his most faithful knights, Edward doubled back and around dusk he rode into Lewes Priory from the south, crashing through the few pickets that de Montfort had set out to stop King Henry slipping away down river. Edward was back, and his first meeting with his father was stormy for the king, rightly, blamed Edward for allowing his men to scatter in pursuit of the Londoners rather than coming back to attack de Montfort in the rear.

However stormy the meeting might have been it did not last very long. Shortly after sunset de Montfort's messenger was back. This time the message was verbal. De Montfort sought a truce and discussions with the king about the future governance of England. Henry agreed, Edward sulked and de Montfort was triumphant.

The Battle of Lewes was over.

CHAPTER 5
AFTERMATH

F ew battles have been so momentous in their effects as the Battle of Lewes. In the short and even the medium term those involved were too busy with recriminations, revenge and dealing with the immediate crisis to see the bigger picture, but looking back over almost eight centuries we can see how events had reached a major turning point.

In the short term the battle led to the agreement that became known as the Mise of Lewes, by which King Henry promised to abide by certain restrictions on his right to rule. The main provision was that the king could not enact new laws or make important decisions without the agreement of a council of four nobles, and if the nobles split 2 votes to 2 on any issue then they would consult the Archbishop of Rouen, who would have a casting vote. This was only a temporary measure, for Simon de Montfort had drawn up a far more reaching constitutional document entitled "A Form for the Government of the King and Kingdom of England". Just as Magna Carta established the key rule that the king had to obey the law like everyone else, this established the key rule that the king had to consult those he ruled before he made new laws.

Under this extraordinary arrangement the King of England could make laws, raise taxes or appoint officials only with the agreement of a Royal Council of nine members. The Council members had to be born Englishmen as well as being barons or bishops. Furthermore all major decisions of the King and Council had to be confirmed by Parliament. Thus far the de Montfort's arrangement was of a piece with earlier schemes, though the necessity to get agreement from Parliament, as opposed to merely consult, was novel. It was in the composition of the Parliament that the revolution came.

Before 1264 Parliament was composed primarily of the barons and bishops. The king could summon abbots or knights if he wished, but he alone chose which and how many knights and abbots he summoned. Effectively the summoning of commoners to Parliament was simply a way for the monarch to pack the meeting with men he knew would support him. The Parliament summoned in 1264, and which met at Westminster in 1265, was very different.

For the first time it was the people who lived in the counties and towns who chose which knights and citizens went to Parliament. Each shire sent two knights to the Parliament, with the other knights in the county deciding which two of them went. Each city or borough (a town holding a royal charter) sent two burgesses, that is men who owned a freehold property in the town and paid taxes to the town authority accordingly. Just as knights in a shire chose which knights to send, so the burgesses chose which two of their own to send.

Effectively the commoner members of the Parliament of 1265 were elected. It is true that the electorate was very limited - neither peasants nor tenants got a vote - but it was nevertheless a massive departure from the past. Previously the monarch controlled who came to Parliament. Parliament might be consulted, but its prime purpose was to act as a conduit for information from the king to the kingdom. Now the roles had reversed. The act of making the members elected meant that each man came to Parliament to represent his town or county to the king, not to represent the king to his home town.

At first, no doubt, not a huge amount changed. The king was the king and nobles were nobles, while knights and burgesses knew their place. But things had changed, and were changing. Just as wealth was slowly shifting from landowners to business leaders, so power was starting to move from nobles to commoners. It is easy to read too much into the 1265 Parliament with the benefit of hindsight, but even at the time people recognised that something fundamental had happened, and nobody more so that young Edward.

Edward was determined to restore his father, the king to untrammeled power. He did so not only for the sake of his father, but also on his own account for he wanted to inherit a kingdom that he could rule himself. In the months that followed, Edward plotted and bribed, cajoled and flattered. De Montfort, by contrast, acted arrogantly and made the mistake of arguing with the Earl of Gloucester and with the bishops. The end result was that many men abandoned de Montfort and in 1265 he was defeated and killed at the Battle of Evesham by Edward.

But Edward found that in his moment of triumph and revenge, he had actually lost the war. It was not the continued resistance of die-hard rebels at Kenilworth, Chesterfield or Ely that was the problem, it was that society and economics were changing and that a mere king was powerless to stop them. Henry III died in

1272, and when Edward summoned his first Parliament as king he did so in exactly the same way as de Montfort had done. In 1295 Edward summoned a Parliament using a form of words that could have been written for him by Simon de Montfort "what touches all, should be approved of all, and it is also clear that common dangers should be met by measures agreed upon in common". Indeed, in 1295 Edward went further than even de Montfort had done. He allowed Parliament to raise matters of concern to the people, "grievances" as they were known, not just to discuss issues put forward by the king. And the agreement of new taxes to pay for the war with Scotland were made conditional on Edward addressing those concerns. The power to grant or withhold taxes depending on whether or not the monarch did as Parliament requested would become one of the greatest powers that Parliament had.

That Parliament of 1295 was later considered to be the "Model Parliament" upon which all later ones were built. The qualifications for voting were laid down clearly, as were the ranks of noblemen and churchmen who were entitled to attend as of right. The Parliament of 1295 may have codified the rules, but it was that

A modern tomb marks the grave of Simon de Montfort at Evesham, Worcestershire. De Montfort was killed the year after the Battle of Lewes and his body mistreated as that of a rebel and a traitor. However, the common people revered the spot where he had been buried and so the site was preserved.

of 1265 that had established the precedent of election by freeborn Englishmen.

Apart from Edward, who became king, the men who fought at Lewes had varied careers after the battle.

King Henry III was held prisoner by de Montfort until the latter's death at the Battle of Evesham in 1265, after which he was released. At first he followed a draconian policy against the rebels, but was later persuaded to come to terms and so brought peace to England. He was not yet 60 when he was restored to power and outwardly he was healthy and robust, but appearances were deceptive. Perhaps the fall from his horse at Lewes took a greater toll that it had seemed, but Henry entered a sudden decline in health. Before long he was too frail to undertake the more arduous duties of medieval kingship and handed them over to his son, Edward. Increasingly Henry devoted his time to religion, and in particular to building a lavish shrine to his hero St Edward the Confessor in Westminster Abbey. He died in 1272.

Richard of Cornwall was held prisoner by de Montfort and was released only after the defeat of the reformers at Evesham, Chesterfield and Kenilworth. Just months after his release Richard suffered a seizure, probably a stroke, from which he never recovered. He died in 1272 and was buried at Hailes Abbey, his tomb being destroyed in the Reformation of the 16th century.

The Earl of Surrey managed to escape the rebel army at Lewes and fled to France. He returned to England in 1265 and fought for the king at the battles of Evesham and Chesterfield. When Prince Edward became king, Surrey quickly emerged as a favoured noble for diplomatic missions. In 1296 he joined Edward for the invasion of Scotland and fought at the Battle of Dunbar. He returned to England soon after, explaining that the Scottish climate was bad for his health. Edward ordered him back north and in 1297 Surrey commanded the English army that was badly defeated at the Battle of Stirling Bridge. Thereafter he stayed on his estates and died in 1304/ He was buried at Lewes Priory, but his tomb was lost when the priory was closed during the Reformation of the 16th century.

The Earl of Gloucester may have been committed to the programme of reform, but he was still a feudal magnate of the old school. He resented de Montfort's later arrogance and was outraged when de Montfort forbade him to hold a tournament due to some legal technicality. He had expected to gain some personal reward for his part in the victory at Lewes, and was disappointed when this did not happen. He was therefore won over by Prince Edward and in June 1265 abandoned de Montfort. He fought against his old friend at Evesham in August

1265 and is thought to have been close enough to see de Montfort cut down and killed at that battle. Edward made sure that Gloucester was rewarded properly this time, granting him several lordships and new lands in Wales.

When Henry III died in 1272, Edward was away on Crusade. It was Gloucester who marched a small army to London and with the Archbishop of York, who happened to be there at the time, proclaimed Edward to be King of England. This was an important legal precedent for it was the first time that a new king was proclaimed using his position as eldest son of the previous king as the legal grounds for his claim to the throne. Prior to this any male member of the royal family had, in theory at least, been eligible to be the new king.

Gloucester commanded an army during the 1282 invasion of Wales, but was defeated at the Battle of Llandeilo Fawr, and then retired to his estates. In 1291 he quarrelled with the Earl of Hereford and both nobles mustered their men for war. Edward, now King Edward I, was not prepared to tolerate these sorts of private wars and had both noblemen arrested. He had them condemned as traitors and stripped of all their lands, though he pardoned them both and restored their lands to them - albeit with dire warnings that he would be less merciful next time.

Gloucester died peacefully in his bed in 1295 and lies buried in Tewkesbury Abbey. His titles and lands passed to his son, another Gilbert.

Henry de Montfort was made Constable of Dover Castle after the Battle of Lewes. This prestigious post put him in control of a sizeable military force and

King Edward I presides over Parliament. Edward I had hated de Montfort, but recognised that the changes and reforms he had introduced were too strong to be swept away. When he became king, Edward embraced many of the reforms enthusiastically. Indeed, many of de Montfort's ideas - such as the innovation that members of Parliament should be elected - remain with us to this day.

contact with France. When civil war broke out again in 1265, Henry rushed to his father's side. He fought well at the siege of Gloucester, then marched with his father to Evesham. He was killed at the Battle of Evesham.

Young Guy de Montfort stayed close to his father in the months that followed. He fought bravely at the Battle of Evesham and fell badly wounded and unconscious in the closing stages. Taken prisoner, he was kept at Windsor Castle until he managed to escape in 1266 and fled to France. Once fully recovered, he took service with King Charles of Naples and distinguished himself as a talented military commander. Charles rewarded Guy by making him Count of Nola, a small town near Naples.

On 13 March 1271 Guy and his brother Simon were attending church in Viterbo when they spotted among the congregation Henry of Almain, son of Richard of Cornwall. It had been this Henry who had hacked the head off the body of Simon de Montfort at Evesham, and who had dragged the wounded Simon the younger to his death. The two brothers dashed forward, drawing their swords. Henry spotted them and dashed for the altar, shouting for mercy. "You showed my brother no mercy," replied Guy who then hacked Henry to pieces, his blood splattering over the altar. Guy was excommunicated for the killing, but Charles retained his services. Guy died in 1288 after being wounded in battle fighting for King Charles.

ALSO AVAILABLE IN THIS SERIES